Heroes and Villains

Write like an Author – Course Book Two

Brian Falkner

Falkner Books
2016

This edition published in 2016 by

Falkner Books

Copyright © 2016 by Brian Falkner

Illustrations by Ron Leishman
Some images in this publication used under 'Fair Use' for educational purposes

On the web at:
brianfalkner.com
writelikeanauthor.com

All rights reserved. This book or any portion thereof may not be reproduced or used in any manner whatsoever without the express written permission of the publisher except for the use of brief quotations in a book review or scholarly journal.

First Printing: 2016

ISBN 978-0-9944567-1-7

Welcome Back!

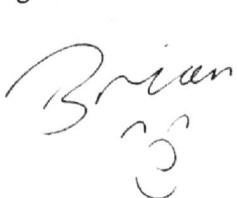

Hi again.

This workbook is all about characters and conflict. These things are the real heart of your story.

I can't stress enough how important both characters and conflict are to a story.

Let's talk about characters for a moment. Characters are what stories are all about. There would be no point in a story without characters.

Think about a murder mystery. Somebody was killed. The point of the story is to find out *whodunnit*. But there are thousands of murder mystery stories. Surely once you have seen a detective solve a murder, you have seen them all. What makes one different from another? The answer is, of course, the characters: the detective; the suspects; even the victim. If they are fascinating and intriguing then the story will be fascinating and intriguing.

In this workbook we will concentrate on developing interesting, engaging, fascinating, likeable (or detestable) characters.

If you get this part right, the reader will love your story.

Happy writing!

Brian

MY CHARACTERS

Here are a few of my favourite characters from my own books.

Jason, *The Flea Thing* - a loyal friend.

Vienna, *Brainjack* - she's a tough nut, but there's more going on beneath the surface.

Cecilia, *Northwood* - thoroughly likeable and brave.

Monster, *Recon Team Angel series* - strong, uncouth and surprisingly intelligent.

Heloïse, *Battlesaurus series* - wild, yet vulnerable.

Who are your favourite characters from my books?

Characters

Readers don't fall in love with stories. They fall in love with characters. This is why when we think about great, memorable stories, it is always the character that we think about.
- Harry Potter
- Shrek
- Matilda
- Katniss
- James Bond
- Buzz and Woody
- Winnie the Pooh

There are so many more.

How can you create a great, memorable character, who the reader will love? Well that's not easy. But I am going to give you some tips to lead you in the right direction.
Let's start with a couple of exercises.

Exercise: Study your buddy

Look at your writing buddy. (If you don't have a writing buddy, just do this to the next person you see.)
Try and notice something interesting about them. The way they cut their hair. That funny mole on their ear that looks a bit like Texas. The way they tied their shoes.

Now write down three things you saw. (Hey, don't be mean. Don't say anything derogatory or disrespectful, we're all friends here.)

Write your three things here:

PROTAGONISTS ANTAGONISTS

As we talked about in the first workbook, heroes are called protagonists and villains are called antagonists.

Why not just say heroes and villains?

Because when we say 'hero' we assume that the character is heroic but often they are not. Some main characters are far from heroic.

And when we see the word villain, we assume they are evil. But many antagonists are not evil. Some are misguided, or mistaken, some are just trying to do the best for their loved ones, but it just so happens that their goals conflict with those of the main character.

Even so, I like to use 'hero' and 'villain' because they are simpler words. Just remember that heroes aren't always perfect and villains aren't necessarily evil.

Exercise:
Tell us something interesting

Now think about yourself. Think about things that people can't see when they look at you. Think of things that nobody would know about you (or at least that not many people would know). Here are some examples, but don't limit yourself to these:
- Do you stand on one foot while you brush your teeth?
- Did you break an arm when you were younger?
- What weird things are you afraid of?
- What odd things do you really love?
- What is your secret heart's desire?
- What strange habits do you have?
- What's the closest you have ever come to being killed?

Write your three things here:

You may have noticed something, doing those exercises. The second exercise is by far the more interesting one.

We really like to find out what makes people tick. What interesting quirks and hates and fears and desires they have. That's way more interesting than what they look like.

Obviously there are exceptions to this rule. For example the way Shrek looks is a big part of his character. He just wouldn't be the same if he was a small, skinny human. But even with characters like Shrek, it is his personality that makes us fall in love with him, much more than the way he looks.

ABOUT BRIAN

Here's some stuff you might not know about me.

I have a line on both my palms called a simian crease' (google it).

I once (accidentally) had my photo in Time magazine.

I appeared on the TV show 'Wheel of Fortune' and was a carry-over champion.

I can say 'hello' in at least one language from every country in the world.

I once wrote a romance novel (it was never published).

Develop your Characters

Think about your main characters. Your heroes, helpers and villains. Use the **character worksheets** *(pages 12-14)* to write at least three things about the way they look; their personality; their situation and their history. Notice that I said 'at least' three. You don't have to stop at three. You can write as many as you want.

Contradictions

Make one of the main traits of your character a contradiction. For example, your character is brave, but is terrified of cats. Or they are strong, dynamic and forceful in public, but in private are insecure and nervous.

Contradictions like these help created a rounded character.
All of this hard work you are doing right now, is helping you create an interesting, believable character. It makes them seem real, and that is the most important thing you can do.

* Tip. While you are thinking about your characters' quirks and personality traits, try to think of how those traits will affect the story. For example, if a character is brave, that should change the story in some way. If they are a coward, that should change the story in a completely different way.

CHARACTER EXAMPLES

Hero:
Your main character. Also known as the protagonist.
- Harry Potter
- Katniss Everdeen
- Shrek

Helper:
A 'sidekick' character who assists the hero.
- Samwise Gamgee
- Donkey
- The Tin Man

Villain:
AKA the antagonist. They work against the hero.
- Lord Farquad
- Smaug
- Voldemort

Minion:
The villain's helper character.
- Orcs
- Death Eaters
- Minions (the little yellow ones)

Being Real

The more you get to know your character, the more real they seem to you.

If the character doesn't seem real to you then they won't seem real to the reader.

Get to know your characters. Get to love them (or hate them). Spend time with them by thinking about them and thinking about what they might do in certain situations.

- How would they react if they found a wallet in the street?
- How do they get on with their mum and dad?
- What scares them?
- What excites them?
- What embarrasses them?

The more time you spend thinking about a character, the more they come alive in your mind, the more they seem like a real person, and not just someone you made up for a story.

You know they have really come alive when your character says things that surprise you. I once had a character say a word I didn't know. I had to go and look it up in the dictionary (scary huh!).

All this stuff about being real is super important, because it is the first step on the path to having your readers care about the characters.

DEVELOPING CHARACTERS

You need to develop your character the same way an artist would. Slowly, bit by bit, until the true personality starts to emerge.

Caring

One of the most important things you must do as a writer is to make the reader care about your characters. If the reader cares about the characters, then they care about what happens to them. But if they don't care about the characters, then why bother reading the story.

To illustrate how important this is, imagine yourself in this scenario:

You are staying in New York in a hotel room with a view of Central Park. Looking out of the window, you see a businessman walk into the park. He looks late for work. He is so busy looking at his watch that he hasn't seen what is all around him: Zombies! You shout and wave, but he doesn't hear or see you. What can you do? Nothing! All you can do is watch as they close in.
How does this make you feel?

- Guilty?
- Frightened?
- Helpless?
- Shocked?
- All of the above?

Now imagine that the person who walked into the park wasn't just some random businessman, but was your eight-year-old sister. How do you feel now?

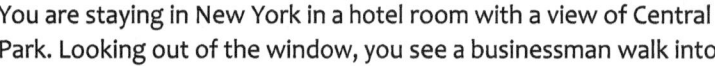

All those feeling are intensified. A hundred, maybe a thousand times stronger. Why? Because you care more about your own little sister than you do about some guy you've never met. That's what stories are like. If you care about the character, then the feelings you experience are far stronger than if you don't.

And as we discussed earlier, emotions (feelings) are what stories are all about.

STEPHEN KING

Really scary books succeed because we come to know and care about the characters. I like to say, "It's the people, stupid, not the monsters!"

- Stephen King

Three Shortcuts to Caring

If there was a secret to getting readers to fall in love with your characters, then I think every author in the world would want to know it. It's a little bit luck and a little bit magic. But it's also a little bit of understanding what makes us tick, and what traits we admire and like in a character. When we like a person, we care about them.

Here are three things that we instinctively like in a person.

1. They are funny

We like people who make us laugh, and we care about people we like. If your character can make us laugh, we will be on their side from the very beginning. They might do something funny, say something funny, or just think something funny.

How can your character be a little funny?

2. They are an underdog

Underdog characters are:

- Vulnerable
- Humble
- Brave

An underdog character is victimised, bullied, powerless, disadvantaged by their circumstances and people around them. They must find the strength to rise up and overcome.

Everybody likes an underdog. That's why so many characters in books for young people are underdogs (I have listed a few of them in the side panel).

Can your character start your story as an underdog?

UNDERDOGS

- The Wimpy Kid
- Bilbo Baggins
- Frodo Baggins
- Katniss Everdeen
- Harry Potter
- Matilda
- Stanley Yelnats
- Ender Wiggin

There are many more!

3. They are nice

A Hollywood consultant named Blake Snyder wrote a book for screen-writers called *Save the Cat*. It was full of really good advice for all writers.

His main idea was this: Early in your story, have your character do something nice for another character.

Simple huh!

We like people who do nice things for others (and we care about people we like). So if we see your character do something nice we will instinctively like them.

It is the easiest of these three traits to achieve in a story, and I think also the most powerful.

What small thing can your character do to show the reader what a good person they are?

Combine these traits

If one of these three traits would help create empathy, how about combining two or three of them.

In The Hunger Games, Katniss is not only an 'underdog', but she really 'saves the cat' when she volunteers for the reaping to save her sister's life.

Use the Character/Trait/Action worksheet on page 16 to plan how you can make (and show) your character being a good, funny underdog, or some combination of the above.

BRIAN SAYS

I was once on a train in Brisbane, which broke down. There was going to be a long delay.

An elderly lady used the emergency intercom and asked to be let off the train to use a payphone. She wanted to call her son to let him know she would be late. The train driver apologised, but nobody was allowed off the train until the problem was fixed.

I offered the lady my mobile phone and refused to take any money for the call. She was extremely grateful, although to me it was a very small thing.

But afterwards, most of the other passengers near me made eye contact and gave me a smile or a nod.

I had gone from being an anonymous stranger, to someone they felt was a '*good person*'.

Other Character Traits

Here are some other common character traits. Use a highlighter pen to mark the traits that apply to your hero. Use a different colour for your villain, and a third colour for other characters.

Absent-minded Active Adventurous Affectionate Aggressive Alert Ambitious Amiable Angry Annoyed Anxious Apologetic Appreciative Argumentative Arrogant Attentive Awkward Bashful Boastful Bold Bossy Brainy Brave Bright Brilliant Calm Capable Carefree Careful Careless Caring Cautious Charismatic Charming Cheerful Clever Clumsy Cold-hearted Compassionate Conceited Concerned Confident Confused Considerate Cooperative Courageous Cowardly Crafty Creative Critical Cruel Curious Dangerous Daring Decisive Demanding Dependable Determined Devious Devoted Discontented Discouraged Discreet Dishonest Disillusioned Disloyal Disorganized Disparaging Disrespectful Dreamer Eager Easy-going Encouraging Energetic Enthusiastic Evil Excitable Expert Exuberant Fair Faithful Faithless Fearful Fearless Feisty Ferocious Fidgety Fierce Finicky Foolish Forgetful Forgiving Fortunate Friendly Frustrated Fun loving Funny Fussy Generous Gentle Gives up easily Glamorous Gloomy Graceful Greedy Grouchy Gullible Happy Hard-working Hateful Helpful Hesitant Honest Hopeful Hopeless Hospitable Hot-tempered Humble Humorous Ignorant Imaginative Immature Impatient impolite Impulsive Inconsiderate Inconsistent Indecisive independent Industrious Innocent Insecure Insincere Insolent Intelligent Intolerant Intrepid Inventive Jealous Jovial Joyful Keen Kind Lazy Leader Liar Light-hearted Lively Logical Lonely Loud Lovable Loving Loyal Malicious Mature Mean Messy Meticulous Mischievous Miserable Moody Mysterious Nagging Naïve Naughty Neat Nervous Obedient Obliging Observant Optimistic Outspoken Patient Peaceful Persistent Persuasive Pessimistic Picky Pitiful Playful Pleasant Polite Popular Positive Proud Quick-tempered Quiet Rational Reasonable Reckless Relaxed Reliable Religious Reserved Resourceful Respectful Responsible Risk-taking Rude Ruthless Scheming Scruffy Secretive Self-centred Self-confident Selfish Sensitive Serious Shrewd Shy Silly Sincere Smart Smelly Sneaky Softhearted Spoiled Stern Stingy Strict Strong Stubborn Studious Supportive Suspicious Sweet Talented Talkative Thoughtful Thoughtless Timid Touchy Tough Trusting Trustworthy Truthful Uncoordinated Undependable Understanding Unforgiving Unfriendly Ungrateful Unkempt Unkind Violent Wicked Wild Wise

MY STORY

Jason is:
- Nervous
- Courageous
- Determined
- Devoted
- Rebellious
- Mature
- Rational

Charli is:
- Feisty
- Mischievous
- Adventurous

The mother is:
- Sensitive
- Withdrawn
- Fidgety
- Anxious

The building manager is:
- Unkempt
- Smelly
- Devious
- Sneaky
- Evil

I might add to this list as I get to know the characters better.

Character Quiz

Can you name these characters from the description of their character traits.

1. She is an over-achiever, very logical, upright and a good person. Very intelligent and a bit of a know-it-all, but also a bit insecure and afraid of failure. She is a very good student. She has brown hair, pale skin and brown eyes.

2. She is helpful and kind, optimistic and a bit of a chatterbox. She has a heart of gold but she has a very poor memory which hinders her ability to help the main hero. She is playful and easily distracted. She can be naive and oblivious to what is going on around her.

3. He is funny and a bit needy, wanting other people to like him. He cannot stop talking, even when it might get him in trouble. He has a very short attention span and acts like a troublesome child. He can be very irritating. But in times of trouble he will stand by his friends. He is very happy-go-lucky.

4. He is suave and cool, even in the most dangerous situation. He is used to danger and pain and will push himself forward against unimaginable odds. He knows how to dress well, he is a connoisseur of fine wine and food. He carries a gun and has a dangerous job that takes him all over the world, meeting deadly foes and beautiful women.

5. He is curious and adventurous, always looking for fun stuff to do. He laughs in the face of danger. He is foolishly brave and too arrogant for his own good. He runs away from his responsibilities due to feelings of shame and guilt.

CLUES

1.

2.

3.

4.

5.

Character Worksheet (Main Character)

Name: Jason Schott	Age: 12	(Male) / Female / (Human) / Animal / Other

Describe them physically	Draw them (if you want)
Jason is small for his age, but strong and wiry. He has light sandy hair cut that sticks up in all directions. He has a missing tooth, the last of his baby teeth which only fell out a week ago and he is waiting for the new tooth to come through.	
Describe their personality Jason has had to grow up quickly because his father spends a lot of time away on business and his mother struggles to cope. Jason sometimes resents having to be the mature, responsible one. He is a caring and devoted big brother to Charli, even though they fight a lot. He suffers from a terrible fear of heights, and another fear of enclosed spaces, or being trapped.	

What are their circumstances?
Jason lives in an old apartment building. His father works overseas. His mother often gets very stressed, and withdrawn. His family is not rich, but can afford the things they need. Next year Jason will go to high school. This scares him. He has a couple of close friends at school, Luke and Artie, but they are going to a different high school.

What are some interesting or unusual things about them?
He doesn't like ice-cream. He eats peanut butter with a spoon.
He has a slingshot which he made himself.
He loves drawing. He also loves reading graphic novels and one day would like to make one of his own.

What has happened in their past?
Jason had a twin brother, Nathan, who died after falling out of a window. This is why Jason is so scared of heights. They used to live in Canberra where his father worked for the government. They moved after the accident.

Character Worksheet (Hero)

Name:	Age:	Male / Female / Human / Animal / Other
Describe them physically		**Draw them (if you want)**
Describe their personality		

What are their circumstances?

What are some interesting or unusual things about them?

What has happened in their past?

Character Worksheet (Villain)

Name:	Age:	Male / Female / Human / Animal / Other
Describe them physically		**Draw them (if you want)**
Describe their personality		
What are their circumstances?		
What are some interesting or unusual things about them?		
What has happened in their past?		

Character Worksheet (Helper)

Name:	Age:	Male / Female / Human / Animal / Other

Describe them physically

Draw them (if you want)

Describe their personality

What are their circumstances?

What are some interesting or unusual things about them?

What has happened in their past?

Showing Character Traits

It's great that you have got to know your character. But the reader needs to get to know them too. How can you show your character's personality to the reader?

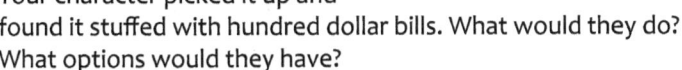

The best way is through action.

Imagine that your character was walking down the street and they saw a man drop a wallet. Your character picked it up and found it stuffed with hundred dollar bills. What would they do? What options would they have?

They could:

- Run after the man and return the wallet.
- Keep the money and throw the wallet in the trash.
- Slip one or two bills into their pocket then return the wallet.
- Ignore the wallet completely.
- There are other possibilities too.

Which one would your character choose?

Whichever one it is, by having your character take that choice in that situation, you reveal their true character to the reader.

You can also reveal character traits through:

Description (You telling the reader what a character is like)

Dialogue (What the character says)

But what a character does (action) is always more revealing than what they say, and much more interesting than you simply telling the reader through description.

This is where we get the phrase **"Show don't tell"**. (More about that phrase later).

ACTION IS CHARACTER

F. Scott Fitzgerald (who wrote The Great Gatsby among many other books) is famous for saying "Action is Character".

When he was writing one of his novels (The Last Tycoon) he apparently wrote these words on every page of his manuscript, as a reminder of their importance.

Everything your character says, but more importantly, everything your character does, reveals a little more of their true personality.

"Action is Character!"

Character Traits/Actions Chart

Use this chart to outline how you will reveal your characters to the reader.

Character	Trait	Action or Dialogue

As an example, here is the start of the chart for my story:

Character	Trait	Action or Dialogue
Jason	Determined/Rebellious	Disobeys his mother and goes to search for his missing sister.
Jason	Nervous	Is increasingly scared by the dark, creepy things he encounters as he goes to look for Charli.
Jason	Devoted	Risks his own life to save his sister.

Character Arcs

The next step in creating engaging characters is to think about how they will change during the course of the story. This is called a character arc.

Let me explain.

Characters change the course of the story by their actions, their bravery, their mistakes and their emotions. In fact everything they say or do affects the story.

But so too does the story affect the character.

Little by little, the events of the story have an effect on the personality of the character.

Think about young Harry Potter at the beginning of that series, and then think about him at the end. He has changed in many, many ways.

Shrek also changes a lot. He starts the first movie as a grumpy, lonely ogre, but by the end he has found love, friendship, peace and acceptance. His life is very different.

As an author, you must not only think about who your character is, but how they will change during the story.

Here write how your character will be different by the end of the story. Keep this in mind as you write the story. Every scene will take your character another step from A to B.

How my character will have changed by the end of the story:

MY STORY

Jason at the start of the story is a fairly innocent character, leading an uneventful life. He does well at school, he takes care of his little sister, he assumes some of the responsibilities of his often absent father. He is on the verge of adulthood.

The events of the story will force him to confront his fears and by doing so, will further his transition from child to adult.

This is a horror / adventure story, but at its core, it is a 'coming of age' story.

Conflict

Characters in conflict is the basis of good stories. Whether they are true stories or fiction. Whether the conflict is with another person, the environment, or even themselves.

We love to read stories about characters struggling with some kind of conflict.

Look at this example

> Judy: I'd like to have red flowers at the funeral.
> Jack: I'd prefer white.
> Judy: Ok, that's fine.

Where's the conflict? There is none.

How could we introduce some conflict? What about this?

> Judy: I'd like to have red flowers at the funeral.
> John: Red? Red!? Are you kidding me? You know she couldn't stand that colour. She was superstitious about it.
> Judy: But white is so traditional and boring.
> John: What are you talking about? This is a funeral, not an art class. Admit it, you're glad she's dead.
> Judy: How dare you! You choose the colour.

Same question, same result, but a lot more drama on the way.

Conflict creates drama, which is the essence of story-telling. It is not interesting to read about happy people doing happy things.

But, as I will explain on the next page, the conflict must relate to the goal or the obstacles.

EXAMPLES

Here are some examples of conflict in popular stories.

Shrek

Shrek wants to get rid of the annoying talking donkey. But Donkey is attached to Shrek.

Star Wars

There is constant conflict between R2D2 and his friend C3P0. This adds interest and humour to the story.

Lord of the Rings

There is conflict between the members of the fellowship of the ring over how to proceed; conflict with Boromir after he becomes affected by the power of the ring; even conflict between best buddies Frodo and Sam.

Conflict → Goal

Most of the conflict in a story comes as the hero tries to overcome the obstacle.

He or she may be in conflict with a villain, with the villain's minions, with the environment or with themselves, but it will mostly relate to the overcoming of the obstacles.

There can be other conflict along the way with characters who are on the same side as the hero. But this conflict should still relate to the goal, and the other obstacles they face.

If two heroes come to a mountain. One wants to go over it, one wants to go around it. Each has very good reasons for their decision. This can be a good conflict scene.

However if our heroes are simply arguing about something unrelated to the main goal, that feels like conflict for the sake of conflict.

For example if our two heroes were arguing about what colour the moon was. Or whether cats made better pets than dogs. Or the personal hygiene habits of one of them. This may sound silly but I have seen it many times in books, movies and TV shows. As if the writer knew they needed conflict but didn't realise that it must always relate in some way to the goal.

Keep your conflict always focussed on the goal, even if it is between two heroes, or a hero and a helper. Otherwise it will seem unnecessary and artificial.

MY STORY

Obviously Jason will be in conflict with the building manager, and the ghosts. But I also want there to be conflict between Jason and his mother.

I will do this by putting them in conflict over Jason's actions.

Jason wants to go searching for his sister. He is desperate to help.

His mother is terrified of losing her son as well as her daughter. She doesn't want him to go.

Both points of view are perfectly reasonable, but it puts these two characters in conflict.

Conflict Role-playing

With your writing buddy, choose one of these scenarios.

One of you take the first line. Your buddy must **agree** with everything you say, and you must agree with everything they say.

> **Scenario One: Rude Student**
>
> A student is sent to the headmaster's office for being rude and disrespectful to a teacher.
>
> First Line: "This behaviour is unacceptable!"

> **Scenario Two: Nuclear Submarine**
>
> The captain and first officer on a submarine have just received a coded order from the president to fire a nuclear missile.
>
> First Line: "On my command, insert your firing key."

> **Scenario Three: Terrible birthday present**
>
> A boy has just bought his girlfriend the worst possible birthday present. It is the last thing she would want.
>
> First line: "You shouldn't have. No you really shouldn't have."

> **Scenario Four: Not enough oxygen**
>
> A spaceship is returning to Earth after being hit by a meteoroid. There is only enough oxygen for one of its two crew-members.
>
> First Line: "One of us has got to go."

Now do the same exercise again, but you both must **disagree** with everything the other person says.

Which way creates more tension and drama?

Which way is easier to keep the dialogue going?

BRIAN SAYS

If you don't have a writing buddy you can actually do this exercise by yourself.

On your computer, or tablet, or pen & paper, jot down the name of the first character as if you were writing a play. Then write what they say.

Next write the name of the second character and what they say.

Each time you swap from one character to the other, try to really see the problem from that person's point of view.

Inner Conflict

The best drawn characters have some kind of inner conflict, as well as conflict with the villain, or other people in the story.

Frodo in *The Lord of the Rings*, has a huge inner conflict. His desire for the ring, versus his need to destroy it.

Simba must choose between his responsibilities as the king of his people, and his desire to live a simple life and have 'no worries for the rest of his days.'

Inner conflict makes characters interesting and makes them real.

Secrets

Another kind of inner conflict comes from secrets.

Do you have a secret? Is there something that you would only tell your closest friend, and maybe not even them.

If someone knew your secret that would give them a kind of power over you. They could threaten to reveal it.

What is your hero's deepest secret? What would they be prepared to do to prevent someone from finding out?

If another character (or the villain) did find out, how could they use that information against your hero?

BRIAN SAYS

A really good story has believable characters who we care about, in conflict with other characters we care about, or who we dislike. Often these characters are battling their own inner conflict as well.

Understanding this puts you a long way down the path to being a really good author.

Actually achieving it is something that all professional authors aspire to.

Being Cruel

You are a god in relation to your story. Everything that exists in your story, everything that happens, is created by you.

But you need to be a cruel god. We want to read about people who struggle against adversity, persevere against all odds, face mighty challenges and endure unendurable pain. Here are some ways to be a cruel and vengeful god:

Mission impossible
   Make your character face insurmountable odds
Sit them on the horns of a dilemma (ouch!)
   Two choices. Neither is good.
Take away what they need the most
   Medicine, water, food, air...
The ticking clock
   Whatever they have to do, time is running out.
Beat them up
   Hurt them. Beat them till they scream. Keep beating.
Hurt their friends and loved ones
   Wait... what? That's not fair!
Tricks, lies and deception
   Have other characters lie to them, cheat them deceive them.
Bring them face to face with their darkest fears
   Whatever they are most afraid of, give it to them in spades
Shatter their preconceived notions
   Whatever they thought they knew, was wrong
The reversal
   You think you have succeeded, but you've just made it worse.
Bad decisions
   Have your hero make some really bad decisions.
Turn the environment against them
   Floods, fires, pests, famines, tsunamis, earthquakes, meteorites, volcanic eruptions, snow, rain, tornadoes, lightning...

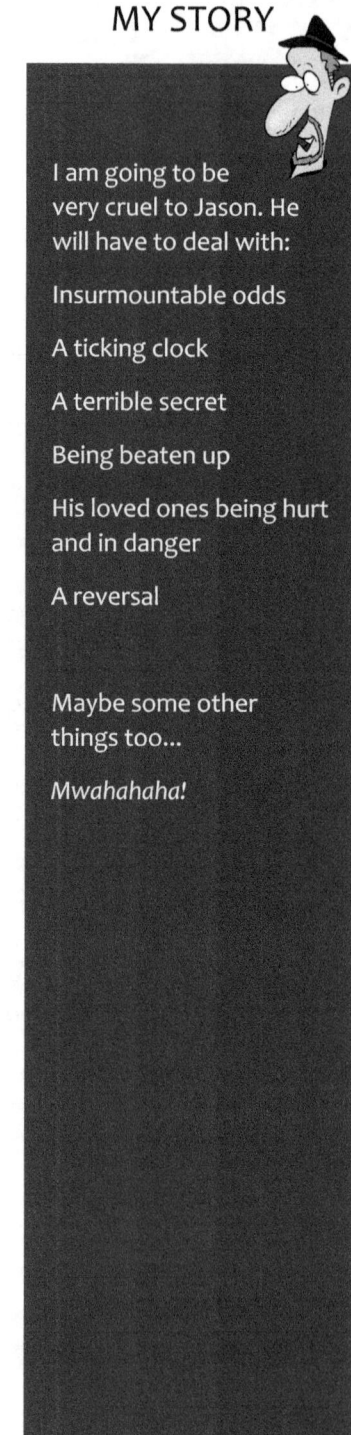

MY STORY

I am going to be very cruel to Jason. He will have to deal with:

Insurmountable odds

A ticking clock

A terrible secret

Being beaten up

His loved ones being hurt and in danger

A reversal

Maybe some other things too...

Mwahahaha!

Character Cruelty Chart

Use this chart to list the bad things you have in store for your characters.

Character	Bad thing

As an example, here are some of the things that will happen to my character

Character	Bad Thing
Jason	The closer he gets to saving Charli, the more beat up he will get. Inanimate objects will try to trip him up, gash his head etc
Jason	He will have to climb onto the outside of the building, despite his paralysing fear of heights
Jason	If he doesn't save his sister before darkness falls, she will be killed.

Answers

Character Quiz Answers

1. Hermione Grainger

2. Dory

3. Donkey

4. James Bond

5. Simba

BRIAN SAYS

One again good work!

That's the end of this character workbook.

The third workbook is all about the process of writing.

It's the next step on your writing journey.

See you there!

Some Character Ideas

If you are struggling with your character *here are some ideas.* You can use these pictures as starting points and flesh them out from your own imagination.

Course Notes:

www.ingramcontent.com/pod-product-compliance
Lightning Source LLC
LaVergne TN
LVHW081528060526
838200LV00045B/2042